JUST DON'T SUCK

CLAY STAIRES
With Comments by Shawn Lowman

ISBN 979-8-9864278-3-6

Copyright 2021 by Clay Staires

Thrive Publishing

Published by Thrive Publishing
3920 W 91st St
Tulsa, Oklahoma 74132

Unless otherwise noted, all scripture quotations are taken from the Living Bible (TLB) copyright 1971 by Tyndale House Foundation. Used by permission of Tyndale House Publishers, Inc., Carol Stream, Illinois 60188. All rights reserved. The Living Bible, TLB and the The Living Bible logo are registerd trademarks of Tyndale House Publishers. Printed in the United States of America.

Contents

I dedicate this book to my wife, Lisa, and two daughters, Maddy and Clare. Knowing the three of you are watching me has made me strive to be a better man - to "Just Not Suck".

THANK YOU FOR THE PUSH!

Endorsement

"Clay Staires has been teaching the concepts from Just Don't Suck to our leadership team at Chick-fil-A for multiple years. He's right on the money, The concepts that he is teaching are things that our young leaders are not learning in schools or at home. It's very applicable if you train leaders or are in a leadership capacity."

ARTHUR GREENO

The owner/operator of two Chick-fil-A restaurants in Tulsa, Oklahoma, an Amazon best-selling author, and holder of two Guinness World Records.

"Clay Staires is an A-Player in every sense of the word. He is kind, giving, purposeful and highly motivated. Through teaching, coaching and now serving in government leadership, Clay is truly living the American dream. If you want to take your effectiveness to the next level, you have to read this book!"

SEAN KOUPLEN

Chairman & CEO Regent Bank, an author and a successful small business investor.

"Clay's ability to speak truth and sprinkle in humor makes this an insightful and entertaining read. Clay's definitions of A, B and C players will change your life trajectory. This book doesn't suck."

DOUG YARHOLAR

Owner & CEO Metal Roof Contractors

"Clay Staires is a dynamic speaker and powerfully practical trainer for business owners. I've seen Clay Staires help to motivate today's employees to perform at their peak in the workplace."

CLAY CLARK

Host of the Thrivetime Show Podcast, Former Oklahoma Young SBA Entrepreneur of the Year, Founder of Several Multi-Million Dollar Businesses, Author and Artist

Introduction

Welcome to the book that I wish I would have read back when I was first entering into the workforce. I wish I had someone giving me the simple, basic steps and tools needed to succeed as I launched out into the competition of the marketplace. I remember finishing my last final at the University of Oklahoma then walking across campus and being struck by the reality of "now I have to get a job" - and almost pooping my pants! Up to this point, I had only worked in my family's business and now I realized that I had to head out on my own and "find a real job". At this point, I sucked! I had a degree, but my mindset about work and how to be successful was totally unreal. Can you relate to this? Did you have a little moment of freak out when you had to figure out how to navigate the process of finding a job, applying for a job, beating all the competition out in the interview to actually get the job? Then there was the terror of starting the job, learning the job and trying to get promoted at the workplace. Making your way in the world can be a very daunting task. That's why I wrote this book.

My name is Clay Staires and my highest desire is to help people navigate successfully through life transitions. This transition into the workforce is easily one of the most difficult transitions that you will go through in your life. However, if you follow the steps I give you in this book, I promise you that you will have great confidence in yourself and you will dominate all the competition when applying for a job or looking for a promotion. It's not rocket science. There are proven moves that I will share with you to help you shine like a star in the universe of employees. Thankfully, you don't suck because you're reading this book but you need to know that most other people suck.

In this book, I'm going to let you in on the secrets that business owners and managers use when they are looking for their next hire. In many cases I'm going to give you advice and information that is the very opposite of what you have heard from your school advisors and college professors. That is because they are wrong and they, for the most part, suck when it comes to knowing how the real marketplace works!

I've been a business consultant since 2012 and I have worked with hundreds of business owners, managers and supervisors and I know what is going on in their heads when it comes to hiring and promoting. I have spoken to thousands of managers and supervisors and they have personally told me what they want and what they look for in an employee, and it's not what most people would think! I have literally heard hundreds of business owners and managers get very emotional as they opened up and talked to me about their frustrations with finding and hiring the right people. In this book, I'll share with you what those doing the hiring have said. It's like getting every answer to every question on a test, before you take it! It's like the ultimate competitive advantage.

In this book, I will give you the proven practical and powerful keys to get any job you're qualified for and even some you may not be qualified for. I'll show you the exact moves you need to take to get "CHOSEN". Once you get chosen, it will be your responsibility to actually implement these moves. I'm confident that you will because you are reading this book and have actually made it to the bottom of page one!

I'm glad you've found this book because I know it will be a game changer for you. The masses don't know these secret tips and hacks. Most people are out there lost in the masses of the status quo and most people are beige and unmemorable in the marketplace. However, this book starts right off in Chapter 1 telling you about the playing field you're on and what your competition looks like. Chapter 2 will give you the best basic business language to use in conversations so you don't look or feel stupid when talking to business owners and managers. Chapter 3 will reveal to you how A-Players think about work and why they always get preferential treatment. Chapter 4 dives into the steps you need to take to find a job and apply for a job that you will love. Chapter 5 will teach you how to dominate the job interview and how to become the best candidate for the job. Once you get the job, Chapter 6 gives you all the tips and hacks to set yourself apart from everyone else in the workplace. Chapter 7 then explains the Employee Evaluation process and you'll learn how to consistently rock the evaluation and Chapter 8 is huge! In this chapter you'll learn how to get promoted in the company and move up to more responsibility and to more pay. In Chapter 9 we'll spend some time going into more detail about the journey of finding the ideal job for you. Finding "the right long-term job" will take some time. There is a lot of discovery that needs to take place before "that job" will present itself to you. However, this book will help you prepare and position yourself for the dream job when that job comes along.

"Knowledge without implementation is meaningless."

THOMAS EDISON, AMERICAN INVENTOR

Finally, I want to introduce Shawn Lowman to you. Shawn has worked for me for the past 3 years and he is an A-Player employee. Shawn was a welder as well as a guy going door to door selling roof repairs before he joined the team. He had big debt, low pay, and a job that required sweaty work that he didn't like. However, he had a dream and passion for something more. Since day one, Shawn has proven himself to be an A-Player. Really, he does it every day... CONSISTENTLY! I've asked Shawn to add some personal stories to this book so you can hear what the path looks like from someone that has used these tips and hacks taught in this book. Shawn is currently a business consultant with me. He coaches over 20 clients with a combined revenue of over $40 million, and he's only 28 years old! His consistent A-player mentality is what has helped him hit his goals of getting out of debt, buying a home, buying a new car and making over $100K a year. All of these changes have happened for him over the last 3 years. Shawn doesn't suck!

So, are you still reading this introduction? Most people don't take the time to read the introduction to books. Especially in "self help" books like this. I never did, but I never read books because I sucked! But for those courageous souls who have taken the time to read this introduction and even the acknowledgments at the end, congratulations! Let's finish this introduction with a quick quiz!

Clay's Checklist of Suckery

Put a checkmark by the ones you can relate to.
FYI - I came up with this list from the things I used to do!
Remember, I used to Suck!

☐ Think that work is a drain
☐ Getting up early is a drag
☐ Complain about pay
☐ Spend more money than you make
☐ No money in your savings
☐ Broke down car
☐ Don't repair car when it breaks
☐ Expired car tags
☐ Too much credit card debt
☐ Still renting my living space
☐ Taking naps at work
☐ Frustrated because "I deserve more"

☐ No Daily To-Do list
☐ No daily schedule
☐ Quit a job so I could go on vacation
☐ Bounced Checks
☐ Late Fees
☐ No Insurance
☐ Car Impounded
☐ Owe money to family members
☐ Driving grandparents car
☐ Thrift store furniture
☐ Call in sick so I can sleep in
☐ Get mad when corrected

CHAPTER 1
YOUR PLAYING FIELD

Back in 2015 when I was still doing a lot of workshops with college-age students, I surveyed hundreds of people using just one question, "What words does the older generation use to describe your generation?"

I'll never forget how it all started. It happened one evening while talking to a class of about 35 students at a local Christian college in Tulsa, Oklahoma. I had asked them this question and was writing each of their answers on the whiteboard -

- Lazy
- Disappointing
- Don't want to work
- No work ethic
- Entitled

- Don't want any responsibility
- Not dependable
- Living in a dream
- Unrealistic expectations
- Disrespectful

There were several more negative descriptions, but I think you get the point. It's worth noting that nobody ever gave me anything positive. It was always negative! I didn't ask for just negatives, but that's the response they gave me when I asked them, "What words do the older generation use to describe your generation?"

After writing about 20 or so adjectives on the whiteboard, I turned to the students and said, "If you want to win in the workplace and dominate your competition, just don't suck!" The class cracked up laughing. I instantly realized I was speaking at a Christian college so I turned to the professor for approval to say, "suck". She wasn't sure, but she didn't shut me down. So I said it again, "Just Don't Suck! That's the wisdom I have for you tonight, Just Don't Suck. Say it with me, Just don't suck. Just don't suck." We started a chant that I eventually had to shut down because it was getting pretty loud. That's the message I have for you in this book. Your competition has such low expectations for their work ethic and your future bosses have such low expectations of their employees. Most humans suck at most things! If you don't believe me, check these stats out...

The Great Hall Of Suck!

75% steal from their boss

https://www.forbes.com/sites/ivywalker/2018/12/28/your-employees-are-probably-stealing-from-you-here-are-five-ways-to-put-an-end-to-it/?sh=481c91913386

85% hate job

Gallup.com - https://returntonow.net/2017/09/22/85-people-hate-jobs-gallup-poll-says/

85% lie on resume

Inc.com - https://www.inc.com/j-t-odonnell/staggering-85-of-job-applicants-lying-on-resumes-.html

68% disengaged at work

Inc.com - https://www.inc.com/sonia-thompson/68-percent-of-employees-are-disengaged-but-there-i.html

70% of the American Workforce either hate their job or are completely disengaged. -

Gallup Poll - https://news.gallup.com/opinion/chairman/212045/world-broken-workplace.aspx

71% of employees are looking for a new job while in their current job

https://www.inc.com/ben-fanning/71-percent-of-employees-are-looking-for-new-jobs-5-strategies-to-address-your-pain.html#:~:text=According%20to%20a%20recent%20study,the%20pursuit%20of%20something%20better.

Americans watch an average of 5 hours of TV a day

https://www.nytimes.com/2009/03/27/business/media/27adco.html

Americans spend 3 hours a day on Social media

https://www.entrepreneur.com/article/307969

40% of employees called in sick when they weren't

https://www.fox9.com/news/survey-40-percent-of-people-call-in-sick-to-work-when-they-arent

This is your playing field. This is who is lining up against you on the other side of the line of scrimmage. I call this vast majority of mediocre humans "Sucking Consumers". These are the people that go to work every day and get paid for being busy but not ever producing anything. I was a school teacher in the public school system for 15 years, trust me, I know there were many teachers who sucked! You know it too because you had them as your teacher in class. There were those few teachers that you'll never forget because they were awesome and inspired you, but many teachers are unremarkable and even poor at their job. It's the same everywhere and in every industry.

So, the answer is really pretty simple... **If you want to be successful, Just don't suck!**

Action Items

» Show up for work 15 minutes early, which is code for on time.

» Don't always have an excuse for your "suckiness."

» Do the job that you're getting paid to do.

» Don't bring your personal drama to work with you.

» Don't sleep with coworkers or customers.

» Don't watch porn at work. 63% of men and 36% of women admit to viewing porn at work.

(https://www.prnewswire.com/news-releases/2014-survey-find-out-how-many-employees-are-watching-porn-on-company-time-271854721.html)

» Don't lie. 85% of job applicants lie on their resume.

https://www.inc.com/jt-odonnell/staggering-85-of-job-ap-plicants-lying-on-resumes-.html

» Don't steal at work. 75% of employees admit to stealing from work.

https://www.forbes.com/sites/ivywalker/2018/12/28/your-employees-are-probably-stealing-from-you-here-are-five-ways-to-put-an-end-to-it/?sh=481c91913386

» It's almost like it's one of the 10 Commandments of The Workplace. "Thou Shalt Not Suck."

» Just don't suck!

As a business consultant, I speak with hundreds of business owners every year. "Not having good employees" is one of their top 3 issues 100% of the time.

Just don't suck!

I asked 30+ business owners what they look for in their employees. This is a summary of what they said. Check the boxes of the qualities that you have been told that you possess.

These are all characteristics that cost you no money and that require no degrees! It just requires that you Just Don't Suck!

☐ Dependable	☐ Coachable
☐ Honest	☐ Growth mindset
☐ Consistent Positive Attitude	☐ Reliable
☐ Ability to communicate well	☐ Good work ethic
☐ A good appearance	☐ Always on time
☐ A good work history	☐ Energetic
☐ Self-motivated	☐ Adaptable

Not everyone is a wonderful person. As you enter into the competition for jobs and promotions, you will see a lot of "good looking" people. People that dress right, look right and talk right. Look again at the statistics on the previous pages that describe the playing field that you're on. Remember, almost 8 out of 10 employees are disengaged or actively disengaged at work according to the U.S. Chamber of Commerce.

Because you are reading this book and you don't suck, you may think, "Just don't suck is common sense". You probably know it's not rocket science to define the characteristics of an A-player employee. For the sake of clarity, I have written down some characteristics of winners and strugglers. Circle the characteristics that describe you.

WINNERS

A-PLAYER DESCRIPTION
(TOP 5% OF EMPLOYEES)

» They arrive at work early and stay until the job is done.

» They embrace ongoing learning and don't push back when assigned something that is new and challenging because they like big challenges.

» They hold themselves to a higher standard than management does so they can show that they really don't need a boss.

» They are hungry for more work and more obstacles to overcome.

» They are goal-oriented and want to win.

» They have a growth-mindset that is focused on constant improvement.

» They consistently get their jobs done without broadcasting their emotional state to the room. With these people, you usually can't tell whether they are going through a personal tragedy or have won life's lottery because they will get their work done either way.

» They can't stand to work around B and C players who represent mediocrity and people who are slowing them down.

» They work hard, go over and above and are well-liked and respected. They typically move up the ranks fast.

JUST GET BYER'S

B-PLAYER DESCRIPTION (MOST EMPLOYEES)

» They arrive to work right on time and leave work right on time or two minutes early.

» They push back at the thought of on-going learning and tend to ask if they are going to be paid for the extra effort because "it's not technically part of their job description."

» They hold themselves to the standard that management sets and actively demonstrates. They constantly compare themselves to their co-workers to justify their lack of effort and excellence.

» They don't want more work and they spend any free time they have planning their next vacation.

» They are not goal-oriented and they hope the company wins just enough so that they don't have to look for another job.

» They have a fixed mindset that is based upon their belief that each person is born with a certain amount of skills and that is all there is to it.

» They consistently get their jobs done while bringing their up and down emotions to the workplace each day.

» They love working with other B and C Players who justify their slow pace of work and whom they can go out to eat with and talk to about everything except for how to do their job better.

» They do the 9–5 thing and they do their job well and are generally known as the "good, not great" people.

STRUGGLERS

C-PLAYERS (BOTTOM 10% OF EMPLOYEES)

» They arrive to work 5 to 10 minutes late and always have a traffic-related, personal, or medical excuse.

» They systematically make teaching them so hard that management gives up on them, but doesn't fire them.

» They have no standards and want to do the least amount of work possible during each workday. When you walk into the room, they minimize their social media and their chat programs and pretend to be working.

» They find ways to leave work early every day and to take extended breaks. They fudge on the amount of time it takes for them to accomplish nearly every task and they need to be praised for just doing their job or they will have an emotional breakdown.

» They view success as based largely upon luck and they are actually bitter toward people who are more successful than they are.

» They have a fixed mindset that is based upon their belief that each person is born with a certain amount of skills and that is all there is to it.

» They only work hard when they emotionally feel like it, and they usually don't.

» They do just enough to scrape through, they never volunteer to take on new projects, and have little to no personal accountability or responsibility.

"C Players" suck and deserve to be fired. They consistently experience lifelong struggles! If you recognize some of these characteristics in yourself, then you already have some homework to work on! Don't get offended. I'm trying to help you. If you find some areas that you need to work on, then start today. Don't wait! Those that wait, suck.

....

"Lazy people are soon poor; hard workers get rich."

PROVERBS 10:4 (NEW LIVING TRANSLATION)

....

"Procrastination is the thief of time, collar him."

CHARLES DICKENS, DAVID COPPERFIELD

I call A and B Players, "Contributing Workers". They contribute to the success of the business, the business owner, the team, themselves and even the customer. They produce positive results for the company. These A and B Players are assets to the team. If you ever played sports, you know that there are some players that are assets to the team and others that are liabilities. It doesn't mean they're bad people, it just means they don't help the team win. We all experienced this on the elementary playground when we would line up at recess to pick teams for kickball and some of the C-Players were picked last. Oh, wait a minute, that probably doesn't happen anymore because of all the political correctness out there.

Geeze, so much on the playground could be preparation for competing in the future but the opportunity is lost in an effort to protect our children from disappointment. It's ok to be non-athletic, pick something else to dominate. According to NCAA.org, only 2% of athletes make it to the professional level anyway. So, it seems like strutting around the playground because you dominate third grade kickball isn't a great life plan! If you suck at something, someone needs to tell you, and, I promise you, it won't be your parents. Don't get pissed, get better. Don't get bitter, get better, and choose something else to dominate.

STRUGGLERS HAVE EXCUSES. WINNERS HAVE TROPHIES!

Well, you made it through the first chapter? Most people didn't. Most people get offended and have already gone onto social media to call me names. Again, this was not written to offend you. I'm writing this to help you to dominate the workplace. If you have gotten offended at what you have read so far, that's a sign that it's time for you to improve.

In the next chapter, I want to show you the basics of how business works and why some people get paid more than others in companies.

Thoughts From Shawn

I remember arriving at the group interview at The Thrivetime Show's World Headquarters in the beautiful Jenks, Oklahoma 45 minutes early. I wore my best suit, which was admittedly not the best fitting, however it was all I had at the time, this was a standard my father has always insisted on throughout my working life. When the interview started I was surprised to see that most candidates avoided the front row so that's where I sat. It surprised me how many people had not followed the simple instructions to bring something to take notes on. I was glad that I had come prepared.

During the interview I was surprised how little the other candidates tried to stand out. I chose to stand when the interviewer addressed me directly to ask questions rather than staying seated like everyone else. I was flabbergasted when only 10% of the group had questions for the interviewer when given the opportunity to ask them towards the end. I had nine questions.

The last step of the interview was to turn in an updated hard copy of our resume to the interviewer. I remember being just plain shocked when another 15% of the candidates did not hand in a copy of their resume and just left without saying anything. After handing in my resume, I asked the interviewer for their email so that I could send them a thank you note along with references.

I ended up getting a call back for an additional interview to be the executive assistant for Clay Staires, one of the Thrive15.com online business school mentors and a practicing business consultant. Imagine my surprise when they called me for an opportunity to directly assist a business consultant working with multi-million dollar businesses!

One thing I learned early on from Clay is that, "Most people are lazy and are perfectly willing to settle for 'good' so it is really not that hard to be great." Until that group interview, which was the first I had ever attended, I did not believe him. I thought these things were common sense. I was wrong. This was a revelation for me. If the majority of other people really suck that bad and the simple fatherly suggestions I used got me an offer for a position far greater than the one I applied for, I knew I was going to win. I knew that it was really not going to be that hard to be great instead of just good.

**SHAWN
LOWMAN**

CHAPTER 2
HOW BUSINESS WORKS
(BASIC INFO TO HELP YOU NOT FEEL OR LOOK STUPID)

When we're young, we are taught that meaning comes from relationships. The value we add to others comes by relating to them in a positive way. We bring something of value like humor, adventure, a listening ear, understanding and caring to the relationship just like the other person brings something of value to us. If the other person doesn't bring "enough" value, then the relationship is draining. Can you relate?

In these early life experiences, we learn that value is in the relationship and the way to add value is to spend more time in the relationship doing relationship-building activities, like hanging out playing video games or sitting around the back deck drinking ice tea talking or binge-watching NETFLIX.

Well, this isn't a relationship book. This is a book about business and how you can gain an advantage and win in the marketplace. If you have been misled or tricked into reading this book because you hoped it would improve your relationships, you should stop reading now and go back to watching 3 hours of TV every day like most Americans do.(https://www.bls.gov/opub/btn/volume-7/television-capturing-americas-attention.htm).

The business world is different from the world most people live in. As much as we want our work life to be emotionally stimulating and relationally gratifying, the capitalist business world only survives and thrives in consistent and constant "production" of a specific goal - profits. This is why so many people are offended at the phrase, "It's not personal, it's business." It doesn't mean that relationships aren't valuable in business (they can actually be very beneficial) but business doesn't value the personal relationship above the success of the company (profits). The success of the company (profits) is the #1 concern. Welcome to the workplace. Some of you are saying, "Clay, when you say it like that, it doesn't sound like the workplace is a safe place." Well, It's not! It's a war zone of competition. This is another way to see evidence that a person may suck as an employee. They are always trying to make the workplace a comfortable place and they consistently complain about the overhead music, the temperature, the lighting, and the fact that they don't have high dollar standing desks. They want better furniture and better snacks in the break room. Oh, and they want a breakroom.

In their book, First Break All The Rules - What the World's Greatest Managers Do Differently, that sat on the New York Times Bestseller list for 93 weeks, Marcus Buckingham and Curt Coffman layout 4 Outcomes of a Successful Business. These outcomes are most often misunderstood or completely NOT understood by most employees. Mainly because of the difference in where most people place value.

A business succeeds or fails according to these outcomes. The only things "the marketplace" cares about are these four outcomes. If a business has these outcomes, it can stay alive for another day. If it doesn't, it's dead! And the marketplace can be a fickle and fleeting friend! It doesn't care as much for a fun, enjoyable and relaxing time with others. It focuses on consistent, focused work that leads to these positive outcomes. Fun comes AFTER success in a business. In fact, fun for highly successful people is found in the consistent activities that lead to their desired results. "Fun" is a hidden core value in the companies that I own. It's hidden because if we are accomplishing the other core values of High Energy, Production, Team and Personal Development then we are having fun! If you don't enjoy these core values and if you don't find them "fun" then you probably aren't a good fit for one of my companies.

THE FOUR OUTCOMES OF A SUCCESSFUL BUSINESS

- » Productivity
- » Profitability
- » Employee Retention
- » Customer Service

Even well-established companies can fall prey to the harsh demands of production and fickle demands of the customers. Take these well-known companies below that were once at the top of their game, but are now all bankrupt and out of business.

These once huge companies are now gone! I'm sure they had some very nice people working in their stores, but the marketplace didn't really care! I'm sure their owners didn't think it was fair, but the marketplace didn't care. I'm sure that many employees were very negatively impacted by these businesses closing, but the marketplace didn't care. A business must solve problems that customers are willing to pay them to solve or it will go out of business!! It's not personal.

So, for those people who are looking for a company or a boss who will put their personal needs ahead of the company's needs, you are going to be very disappointed in the competitive workplace. As you begin your search for a job, along with so many others, it's important that you have an understanding of what a business owner/manager MUST HAVE for their business to be successful. Just the fact that you know this and can bring it up in discussion during an interview will put you way ahead of your competition for a job.

In this chapter on How Business Works, it's important to begin with some basic definitions. I know these may seem very elementary, but it's amazing the number of people in business that don't fully understand these concepts. Most people decide to start businesses because they want to help people. This is nice, but helping people, by itself, doesn't last long if you can't make money at it.

"There is only one boss. The customer. And he can fire everybody in the company from the chairman on down, simply by spending his money somewhere else."

SAM WALTON, FOUNDER OF WAL-MART

SO HERE ARE SOME BASIC TERMS TO UNDERSTAND.

REVENUES

The total amount of money that comes into a company due to sales.

EXPENSES

The amount of money that goes out to accomplish the purpose of the company.

PRICE OF ITEM

How much you charge for an item.
What a customer pays.

COST OF GOODS SOLD

How much it costs you to produce/provide that
item. Not just the price a business pays for it,
but also all the other costs that go into creating
that item to customers - i.e. branding, marketing,
advertising, selling, packaging, distributing...

PROFIT (MARGIN)

How much total money you have left after
you sell a product or service after paying all
your expenses.

WORK - PRODUCTION

What do you produce? Activity alone is
not production. You must actually produce
something.

There is a definition of work that I learned from my college physics class
(that I hated!). It states that Work is a measure of the energy expended in
applying a force to move an object from one point to another.

$$\textbf{``W = F x D''}$$

This definition of work is a key term to understand when you step into
working for a company! Work is about what you get accomplished not about
how many hours you showed up for the job. You may feel like you have
worked really hard, but unless you have produced something that the market

is willing to pay for, the marketplace doesn't recognize your effort. In the world of capitalism, you must ensure that the company is generating more revenue per hour than they are paying you. This is what makes you stand out from the competition. Producing desired results for the company is what will get you recognized and promoted so you can earn more money to allow you the freedom to make the decisions you need to make to meet your life goals.

However, effort is meaningless without execution. "I did my best!" The marketplace doesn't care about your best, it cares about whether you can produce something that people are willing to pay for. For you to get a raise or get a promotion and move up the ladder of success you must become a producer.

You don't add value to a business just because you're a nice person and because people like you. You're not adding value to a company just because you stay busy all day wearing all different kinds of hats.

Employees (that's you) add value to a company by doing these three things!

1 Save the company money

2 Make the company money

3 Save the company time

It's a very nice bonus if these employees are also nice people that are easy to be around, but this part is not the requirement. In order to secure a raise, to get promoted and to climb the ladder of success, you must become an expert of saving the company money, making the company money or saving the company time. You are going to be able to do this because you're reading this book and you don't suck!

TIME AND MONEY – This is how you add value in the marketplace!! If you can't do these things, you are not "worth" much for the company. You may be a very nice person with some wonderful personal qualities, but you are not "worth much" to the company and therefore your "security" in the job is very limited.

I would like to take a moment to introduce you to Mark Mason's Disappointment Panda. **The Disappointment Panda** (created by the *New York Times* best-selling author Mark Manson) is a superhero whose superpower is to tell you the harsh truth about yourself – so that you can come to terms with reality and begin to make a real practical plan that can actually help you improve so you can meet your goals as opposed to allowing you to live your life detached from reality chasing magical unicorns and dreams that are not possible to achieve.

MARK MANSON
New York Times best- selling author

The further down the chain of command you are, the more your position is expendable. Meaning, there are many other people that can do what you do, therefore, your pay will be low because the expertise needed to be hired at that level is low.

Minimum wage is for minimum expertise and minimum production value.

Are you paid by the hour? How much work can you get done in an hour? If you can get more work (production) into an hour and solve more problems in an hour then someone else working that same hour, you have "saved" time and therefore saved money for the company. You are more productive than the other worker. Welcome to the wonderful world of being a valuable, contributing worker! You are contributing to the bottom line and the success of the company and positioning yourself for recognition and reward. This is a good thing in a competitive workplace.

On the contrary, if someone (not you) wastes time and works slowly, they can cost the business money and therefore their job security will be called into question. Their boss will find themselves asking if there is somebody else who can do that job better. If they have wasted time AND they have produced less, that's a double foul!

They could soon be promoted to "customer status" in the company (that's code for getting fired).

MORE DEFINITIONS -

There are two primary kinds of organizations (again, very basic stuff here):

NON-PROFIT ORGANIZATIONS

> All revenues go back into the organization to help provide a public service to help more people that often can't afford to pay for these products or services. No profits are generated for the investors, owners, etc.

FOR-PROFIT BUSINESSES

> All profits go to owners or investors (stakeholders). They can then keep the profits as earnings or put money back into the company and/or product to help the company grow and make even more money.

Both non-profit organizations and for-profit businesses must have money to keep going and provide the goods and services. Money is the life blood of any organization. Without money, these companies will shut down and will no longer be able to provide the goods or services or jobs for others. Some people (not you) get offended at this reality because they think the value is primarily found in people, feelings and what's "fair for everyone". You don't think this way because you don't suck and you know that rewards go to the diligent. But many other people do think this way. This is why 9 out of 10 new businesses fail within 5 years. It's not that they don't have passion, it's just that they run out of money because they didn't do the actions necessary to make a profit.

» Non Profit organizations hire employees but also use volunteers to cut down on expenses to help fulfill their mission. They also rely on donations (instead of sales) to help boost their income to help them meet the financial demands of the organization. Sometimes a non-profit will spend more than they bring in but they will make it up with more donations.

» For-Profit businesses hire employees only. If they want to boost their income they must sell more of their product or service or cut expenses. To cut down on expenses they look for more efficient and cost-effective ways to provide their product or service. They can't spend more than they make or else they will eventually go out of business like, JCPenney, Circuit City, American Apparel and the other businesses mentioned at the beginning of this chapter.

As an employee or a volunteer, list 3 ways you add value to a business or organization? This will take some thinking. Don't avoid it. Take the time to think, process and record how you, specifically, can add value to a business or organization.

How can you make the company more money?

_____

How can you save the company money?

_____

How can you save the company time?

_____

It's not just by helping the company bring in more sales or donations. Yes, you can help the company to earn more money but, more importantly, you have to focus on improving the product or service you offer to the customers while simultaneously reducing expenses.

What do For-Profit companies do with their profits? Many for-profit companies have legal responsibilities to fulfill with their profits. They have to pay back investors or pay off bank loans they used to start the company. Many times, these responsibilities can reach up to 70% to 80% of the company's profits. What you think is going into the pockets of your managers and owners is often actually going back to the bank or into the pockets of investors, or to bill collectors.

It's not just about how much total sales a pizza business does. It's how much PROFIT they actually get to keep after paying all the expenses necessary to provide that pizza.

 Sorry, I didn't tell you that math would be involved in this book. Don't freak out. You can do this because you don't suck. Let's say a pizza shop earns $50,000 in one month. How much money is left over after paying for all the pizza ingredients to pay for the overhead expenses like payroll, utilities, rent, insurance and taxes? Most often, what is left over is relatively small compared to the $50,000 made. What is left over is called profit and it goes to the owner who took the risk needed to start the business? For a restaurant, this is usually less than 10%. So on that $50,000, less than $5,000 goes to the owner as profit. That works out to about $60,000 a year.

So you can't just take the price of an item and how many items are being sold and say, "Wow, they are making a lot of money!" They may be selling a lot of pizza, but that doesn't mean they are keeping a lot of money.

By the way, these numbers are great to know. What is the company's weekly and monthly net profits? Knowing this number can help you focus your A-Player activity into improving this number.

OVERNIGHT SUCCESS IS A MYTH

» It took Steve Jobs nearly two decades to become an overnight billionaire. He started his company in 1976 in his parent's garage. The company didn't gain any real traction for 8 years when it created Macintosh in 1984.

» Google was started in 1996 by Sergey Brin and Larry Page but didn't achieve success until 2004 when they went public. It took 8 years of consistent, constant production to become an overnight success.

» Fred Smith first had the idea for FedEx in 1962 but it took him 9 years to turn his "big idea" into a profitable business.

» Bill and Scott Rasmussen had a dream to create the world's first television network devoted to sports back in 1978. However, ESPN's overnight success didn't become profitable until the mid-80's. It took many years of grinding it out each day and producing results for the company before they finally became profitable.

» It took Twitter 12 years of continuous grinding to become profitable and Amazon took 14 years - 58 quarters - to become profitable.

AH! MORE DEFINITIONS!
THIS BRINGS US TO SOME MORE IMPORTANT DEFINITIONS.

BREAK-EVEN POINT

How many items do we have to sell to break even? As an employee, how can you help increase the number of items sold? Ask your manager or business owner how many "widgets" you have to sell to break even. This is a very important number to know and to set as a target for a company. You can show more value by knowing this number. If you don't know and don't care about this number in the company you work for then you suck.

PROFIT PER UNIT

As an employee, how can you lower the cost of the item without sacrificing quality? Ask your manager or business owner how much it costs to sell each "widget". This is a very important number to know and to set as a target for a company. You can show more value by knowing this number. If you don't know and don't care about this number (or don't care about this number), you probably suck.

There's a difference between the money a business makes and the money a company keeps. As you can see just because a business makes $1,000,000 in revenue, doesn't mean the owner gets to keep it. I had a client that owned a restaurant and he made about $800,000 a year in revenues but only 8% of it was profit! MORE MATH!

How much did my client actually get to keep?

Before paying taxes, my client was able to bring in $64,000. However, after paying for state, federal, local and other government imposed fees and permits, my client did not get to keep anywhere near $64,000. All that hard work and risk of being an owner and he pocketed about $40,000 that he then had to pay personal income tax on! WHAT??

By the way, people (not you) who refuse to do this math, just might suck!!

Contributing Workers have a basic understanding of these terms and concepts and this knowledge allows them to contribute more value to the company. Sucking Consumers just show up to work and expect to get paid for the time they spend there. They don't consider "production"; they just think about the amount of time they "spend" at work. They think of "effort" and not "efficiency" and "execution".

Now let's take a look at the 68% of the working population that is disengaged (sucking consumers) and what it's costing companies.

"Gallup estimates that these actively disengaged employees cost the U.S. between $450 billion to $550 billion each year in lost productivity. They are more likely to steal from their companies, negatively influence their coworkers, miss workdays, and drive customers away."

In fact, a report published by CBS News and the U.S. Chamber of Commerce found that 75% of employees actually steal from the workplace.

An article in Inc.com, tells us that the amount of time wasted at work each week is 21.8 hours!

https://www.inc.com/david-finkel/new-study-shows-youre-wasting-218-hours-a-week.html

21 Hours—That's a part-time job!

Holy Cow! Look at what you can save your company (add to the bottom line) simply by being a contributing worker! JUST DON'T SUCK!!

You may be asking, "But Clay, why should I care about how much money the company makes? I'm more concerned with what I need to make!" Ah, if you think this way then you just might suck!

How do you help yourself by adding value to the company? Have you ever said to yourself, "I want a raise?" Why do you want a raise? Most people want a raise because they need or want more money. This makes sense and there's nothing wrong with this. However, many people (not you) justify getting a raise by saying, "I have been here for a certain amount of time and so I deserve a raise." They don't think of the value they add, they just think about the time they have spent on the clock and the effort they feel they have put in.

"It's not about how much money you make, it's about how much you keep."

**ROBERT KIYOSAKI,
BEST SELLING
AUTHOR OF RICH
DAD, POOR DAD**

For them, time equals value. Many people say they should be given a raise because of their loyalty, but, just because you have been at a company for a long time, doesn't necessarily mean you're loyal. It may be tenure or longevity, but it's not necessarily loyalty.

You don't deserve a raise unless you have added value to the company by helping the company save money, make money, or save time.

Remember your pay is directly connected to your position and your ability to positively impact the value of the company. How "replaceable" are you? Let's take a look at the production pyramid.

PRODUCTION PYRAMID

EFFECTIVE LEADER

EFFICIENT MANAGER

CONFIDENT TEAM BUILDER

CONTRIBUTING WORKER

SUCKING CONSUMER

THE PRODUCTION MINDSET PYRAMID

"You can have everything in life you want, if you will just help other people get what they want."

ZIG ZIGLAR, MOST POPULAR MOTIVATIONAL SPEAKER EVER

Low skill workers are immediately **REPLACEABLE** so their pay tends to be low.

Great CEOs are **IRREPLACEABLE** so their pay tends to be extremely high.

But you have to realize that the CEO is not coming to work each day with the same responsibilities as the worker! CEOs have much more responsibility and pressure on them. Even if all you see them do is sit in an office or breeze through the store once a week, the CEO is responsible for making sure that the company makes products and services that customers actually buy while also making sure that they pay their employees a wage that is livable, and yet does not irritate their customers to the point that they feel gouged because the employee pay is so high. Can you imagine what all goes into keeping a business growing while keeping customers and employees happy?

So, do you want to get paid more? Become more valuable! Become irreplaceable! Break out of the status quo! It's not hard! Eight out of ten workers are status quo (sucking consumers). You've got to add value to move up!

How do you stand out and add value at the different levels of production?

THE WORKER - DO YOUR JOB WELL

> This level is the hands on level. Most often this hands on work can be done by anyone so a person working at this level can easily be replaceable.

TEAM BUILDER - HELP OTHER PEOPLE DO THEIR JOB WELL.

Employees at this level have the ability to gather and recruit others to join them in doing quality work. This is a higher level skill and adds more value to the position and the employee. They are a little bit harder to replace. You need to learn this skill so you can add more value to the company.

MANAGER - CREATE SYSTEMS AND HOLD PEOPLE ACCOUNTABLE TO FOLLOW THE SYSTEMS.

Managers are able to think in terms of efficiency and accountability. They see repeatable activities as systems and they require others to follow these systems. Managers are held accountable for ensuring the company/department/team reaches specific goals. Managers are of great value to a company and are hard to replace.

LEADER - SETS THE VISION AND INSPIRES THE ACTION OF EVERYONE DOING THEIR JOB WELL.

Leaders make personal sacrifices for the good of the company, the employees and the customers. When combined with the other levels, the leader is very rare.

This is how you make more money! Add value and increase the bottom line for the company. Stay engaged and intentional about how the company is doing as a whole, and don't be just focused on how much you're getting paid.

"The man who does more than he is paid for will soon be paid for more than he does."

NAPOLEON HILL - THE BEST SELLING AUTHOR OF THINK AND GROW RICH

To finish out this chapter, it's important for you to know what is important to your manager (or owner) in your company. What keeps them awake at night and what are they thinking during the day?

What matters to managers and what doesn't matter to managers in business:

Matters Everyday in the Workplace

» Employees being on time
» Doing what you're told to do
» Earning your wage
» Producing results
» No drama
» Whether you fit into the company culture or not
» Dependability
» Willingness to learn

Doesn't Matter... EVER in the Workplace

» Your video game scores
» Your number of likes or friends on Facebook
» How you feel
» You being inspired and having fun at work
» Your passions
» Whether you're a fun person with a lot of friends
» Your definition of what's fair
» You feeling emotionally safe and cared for

Thoughts From Shawn

Everyone can fall into the trap of performing like a B-Player if they are not intentional. This was true for me at nearly every job that I had worked before getting hired to work with Clay Staires. My mindset was terrible. I had viewed these jobs as if they were just barriers. Working a job was a negative sacrifice I had to make so I could have money to do what I wanted. Work kept me from pursuing loftier goals and hobbies in my life. I would dread going into work everyday. Admittedly this was an initial struggle of mine. As I transitioned out of the mindset of having a job just to pay bills and into the mindset of having a career that could actually help me get to my goals faster I had to endure some uncomfortable conversations with Clay about the differences between A-Players and B-Players. What I have learned from him is that it doesn't matter what your job is, the attributes of an A-Player are only continually accessible to those who understand that work is an asset to your future rather than a mindless task that's done for some "rich boss" who doesn't care. However, now I know that working like an A-Player is only 10% harder than working like a B-Player. I know, I have done both. Being an A-Player is about showing up 15 minutes early and not 5 minutes late.

The lesson here is that until you can view work as a vehicle to help you get where you want to go instead of being a burden; an impediment or a brick wall keeping you from your desires, you will not be willing to put in the slight bits of extra effort along the way that are absolutely required to become a true A-Player.

SHAWN LOWMAN

"JUST DON'T SUCK"

CHAPTER 3
HOW DO A-PLAYERS THINK ABOUT WORK?

What is the employee on the left thinking about work?

What is the employee on the right thinking about work?

"Your beliefs become your thoughts, Your thoughts become your words, Your words become your actions, Your actions become your habits, Your habits become your values, Your values become your destiny."

MAHATMA GANDHI

THE LEADER OF INDIA'S NON-VIOLENT INDEPENDENCE MOVEMENT AGAINST BRITISH RULE.

It all begins with the way you THINK! Early on, as I became a business owner, I heard T. Harv Eker, the best selling author of Secrets of a Millionaire Mind, say, "Your thoughts will grow into your beliefs and your beliefs drive your decisions and actions. Your actions will determine your results." He put up this acronym to help us remember the order -

Remember, according to Gallup, 68% of the American workforce is "disengaged" at work!

https://news.gallup.com/opinion/chairman/212045/world-broken-workplace. aspx

Why? They simply have the wrong way of looking at their work. Most people think work is a "necessary evil" in order for them to get the money they want. Most people choose to view work as something that stands between them and what they want.

Unfortunately, this way of thinking about work will always position you to "avoid" and to "resist" doing meaningful work.

Another way to look at work is as if it were a VEHICLE that allows you to get where you want to go. This may be the way you look at work because you don't suck.

So, if work (your job) is a vehicle, the question becomes, "Is your vehicle moving you toward your desired destination?" Somehow we have to embrace the job/vehicle that we're in today so we can connect with the daily work that is going to get us where we want to go.

Three profoundly true statements that may just hack you off:

>> You have been created for work.

>> Work is good!

>> Work is required to get you where you want to go.

Some people point to the Bible and say that it supports the idea that we were created to hang out as if we're in a garden all day; that "work" is the curse. That's not true. Colossians 3:23-24 says, "Whatever you do, work at it with all your heart, as working for the Lord, not for human masters, since you know that you will receive an inheritance from the Lord as a reward. It is the Lord Christ you are serving." (NIV Version)

Did you know that 3 out of 4 people in America still see the Bible as the Word of God?

Three in Four in U.S. Still See the Bible as Word of God -

https://news.gallup.com/poll/170834/three-four-bible-word-god.aspx

I bring this up because many people have the idea that "work is bad".

The "idea" of work was given before the "fall of man" when God told Adam to work in the Garden;

> "The Lord God took the man and put him in the Garden of Eden to work it and take care of it."
>
> **GENESIS 2:15**

In the original Hebrew language in which the Old Testament was written, they did not have two words for the word work and worship. In fact, both "work" and "worship" mean the same thing. Essentially your "work" was your "worship" to God.

Leisure is purposeless. Yes, it may be really nice for a time to have no responsibilities and to not feel the pressure of producing anything, but before long we actually begin to offend our very nature when we resist work and produce no valuable outcome in the world.

What if we could approach work with this mindset: Work is my best friend and work is my worship. Why? Because work shapes you!

Robert Greene, in his book *Mastery*, gives us his insight on how to think about work. He encourages his readers to "...enlarge your concept of work itself. Too often we make a separation in our lives - there is work and there is life outside of work, where we find real pleasure and fulfillment. Work is often seen as a

"Work Shapes You."

means for making money so we can enjoy that second life that we lead. If we experience this time (of work) as something to get through on the way to real pleasure, then our hours at work represent a tragic waste of the short time we have to live.

Instead, you want to see your work as something more inspiring, as part of your vocation. The word 'vocation' comes from the Latin meaning "to call or to be called". You must see your career or vocational path more as a journey with twists and turns rather than just a straight line."

When work is viewed as a tool to shape you, or when it's interpreted as your calling, then it takes on a very different role in your life. Work becomes necessary for you to fulfill your purpose in life.

Did you know that Harvard Medical School announced that there is a 40% increase in depression within just 27 weeks after retirement? You are meant to live with purpose. Read, "Is retirement good for health or bad for it?"
http://www.health.harvard.edu/blog/is-retirement-good-for-health-or-bad-for-it-201212105625

"All work is noble."

MARIA MONTESSORI
(A lady who lived a long time ago whose work lives forever because she created the Montessori philosophy of education.)

....

"And where I excel is in my ridiculous, sickening, work ethic. You know, while the other guy's sleeping? I'm working."

WILL SMITH

(THE ACTOR, PRODUCER, RAPPER, AND SONGWRITER WHO HAS WON NUMEROUS AWARDS IN TELEVISION, FILM, AND MUSIC.)

Here's a big question that few people are able to answer: What work are you designed to do? Oftentimes we can dislike the work and interpret that as disliking the overall concept of work! It's vital for each of us to discover what work we have been designed to do. We must determine what work aligns with our design.

Work gives meaning, purpose, value, and respect.

CHAPTER 4
FINDING AND APPLYING FOR A JOB

Wow! Are you still reading? You don't suck if you've made it this far without getting distracted by a video game or a boyfriend/girlfriend. This is a good sign! You're the kind of person I love to be around.

So, now that we have a basic understanding of how a business works and how "A-Player" employees think about work, let's jump into some practical steps on how to get out there and find a job.

"The three great essentials to achieve anything worthwhile are, first, hard work; second, stick-to-it-iveness; third, common sense."

THOMAS A. EDISON

(THE FOUNDER OF GENERAL ELECTRIC AND THE INVENTOR OF THE FIRST PRACTICAL LIGHT BULBS, RECORDED SOUND, AND MOTION PICTURES)

Let's start out with a little Personal Preparation

Before you set out on most vacations in the family roadster, you usually start out with a destination in mind. The destination is what determines the path you take. If there is no destination then just roaming around aimlessly is going to be the result. This may be ok for a vacation, but it sucks as a career path. So let's start out with some kind of a destination in mind.

Your destination will determine the level of your determination to stay focused and committed. If the destination isn't valuable enough to you, it will be easy to give up when things get un-fun.

Finally, if you can apply pig-headed determination towards a particular destination over an extended amount of time, you can be sure you will achieve your destiny!

Why are you looking for a job? What is it you hope to gain from getting a job? Money is always a good thing, but if that is the only motivator for you, I promise you will become complacent very quickly and you will eventually say, "They're not paying me enough to do this job." In other words, YOU WILL SUCK!

Your destination will determine your determination. If money is the only destination, then you're determination will be very short lived.

However, what if you could actually look at a job as a resource and as a means to get you closer to the achievement of your goals? Remember in Chapter 3 when we said, "work is a vehicle to get you where you want to go"? Here's a quick checklist for you to consider while you are comparing job opportunities. Remember, this checklist was created for A Players. B and C players would never take the time or expend the energy needed to think about this. Remember, they suck (as workers, and maybe as people, but we won't judge them that far).

Some "Destinations" your job could provide you...

FINANCIAL STABILITY -

Yes, it's important that your job will be able to provide you with the amount of money that you are needing to pay for your financial responsibilities. If you think you would like to stay in this job for an extended period, you will need to ensure that the pay will grow as your responsibilities in life grow. Some people say, "But, Clay, that means I would actually need to sit down and figure out how much money I need and want to make? I don't want to do that. I just want to get a job." Well, these people suck! And they will make a poor employee because they are too shallow-minded. But that's not you. You have made it to Chapter 4 of this book and you don't suck!

SKILL DEVELOPMENT -

This is another great advantage of working in a job. You get to actually learn a skill that you can use to add value to other people's lives. Zig Ziglar once said, "You can have everything in life you want, if you will just help other people get what they want." This is true. This is the secret to life in a capitalist society. It's one thing to know what people want, however, it's a very different thing to have the skills needed to provide it to them. T. Harv Eker, the best selling author of The Secrets Of The Millionaire Mindset gave us the formula for financial success. There are 4-Steps: 1) Define a problem that a lot of people have and would be willing to pay money for the solution. 2) Create a solution. 3) Exchange the solution for money. 4) The more people who want the solution, the more financial success you can have. However, this will require skills on each level of the Production Mindset Pyramid. A job is a great place to learn hard skills like carpentry, accounting, how to make food and much more. This is great because you will learn WHILE GETTING PAID!! I promise you, one of the biggest problems bosses have is finding great employees. You can easily be their solution... just don't suck!

PERSONAL GROWTH -

Each of us is responsible for increasing our capacity so we can process greater complexity. Your life (everyone's life) gets more complicated as you age. There are more and more responsibilities to be accountable for. Use your job as a tool to help you grow personally. Look for, and even ask for, opportunities to learn. Unfortunately, many people never expand their capacity to meet this increasing complexity in life and, as a result, they flatten out (peak) early on and then live most of their lives in quiet desperation - always wanting more and waiting for the big break that never comes. This doesn't make them bad people, they just kind of suck at doing life and at growing and maturing. This is how 85% of other people live their lives at work every day. Can you believe that that's the percentage of people who hate their job? https://returntonow. net/2017/09/22/85-people-hate-jobs-gallup-poll-says/

CONNECT TO INFLUENCERS -

This can be a big differentiator in choosing one job over another. Does this job give you the opportunity to meet people that will be able to help you in the future? According to Ruby Payne, author of A Framework for Understanding Poverty, this type of thinking comes out of a "wealth-class" mindset. Position yourself to gain relationships with influencers who can open doors for you in the future. No matter where you work, I would strongly encourage you to meet and get to know the owner of the company, even if it's a national company like Chick-fil-A. Although you may feel as though you are just "an employee" making money for Dan Cathy with every shift that you work, you are his employee! Write him a letter (multiple letters) and tell him thanks for hiring you. Get his email address and send him an email when you get promoted. Ask him questions. Keep knocking until you get a response from him. In a small company, maybe your boss or the owner is an influencer in the community. Get to know them. Ask them to introduce you to other influencers in the community. If you're an A Player, I promise you, they will be happy to introduce you to these people that will be very helpful to your future.

> **IMPROVE THE WORLD -**
>
> Just like money is a poor end-all goal for you in a job, just thinking about personal gain will most likely leave you feeling a little empty as well. If you can find a job that regularly gives you an opportunity to help people in need, you will quickly find that more than just your hands are engaged at work, but your heart is as well.

3 Questions for you to answer when looking for a job that's right for you:

1. Do you know what you love to do - Passion? It's hard to know when you're young and you haven't had a ton of experiences. Many times a particular job is a great place to learn what you DON'T like as much as learning what you do like.

A-Players see work (and the job) as an opportunity. C-Players see work as an obstacle that's in the way of getting what they want.

It took multiple jobs for me to learn what I was really good at, what I really loved and what I could actually make good money doing. It takes a while to learn these things. Remember the statistics in Chapter 1 - 68% of employees are "disengaged at work". These are simply employees that stopped growing or they have allowed themselves to get stuck in a job that no longer challenges them to grow. Maybe they loved it at one time, but, over time, they have come to hate it (or hate themselves - but that's a deeper subject).

2. Do you have skills - Purpose? If you're young and inexperienced in the working world, you probably don't have a lot of valuable skills. You may have knowledge from getting a degree but you still lack the practical experience that develops skills. This is why your paycheck is lower than other people that have acquired skills. Use your job to gain marketable skills that will help you grow into your future. If the opportunity comes up, let the company pay for your skill development. Go to workshops, trainings, classes, seminars, and other skill building activities.

3. Will people pay you for your skills - Profits? It's great that you can beat all your friends in Call of Duty or Super Smash Bros, but unless you have figured out a way to get paid a lot of money for it, it just doesn't matter. Develop skills that people will pay money for. We call this a "marketable skill". These skills are discussed more in Chapter 6.

To find a job that combines your passion, your purpose and profits is what Lance Wallnau, speaker, author and current director of Lance Learning Group, calls reaching "Convergence". If you can find something you love, that you are highly skilled at and that people will pay money for, you have won the game of life.

However, most people can get stuck in compromise and, rather than continuing to press forward to obtaining all three (passion, purpose and profits), they settle for just obtaining one or two. But that's not you! You are an A-Player!

APPLYING FOR A JOB

This really is where the Pig-Headed Determination of an A-Player really pays off.

What if you apply for a job and they say, "No". What would happen if you applied again? What would happen if you showed up again? What would happen if you didn't take, "No" for an answer?

Remember all the statistics from Chapter 1. With this in mind, I promise you that most employers out there have at least one employee that they would love to fire TODAY! The reason why they don't is because they don't have someone to replace them with. That means there is an opportunity for an A Player to move in.

CHAPTER 5

INTERVIEW LIKE A ROCK STAR

According to Forbes.com, 33% of bosses know within 90 seconds of an interview whether they will hire someone.

https://www.forbes.com/sites/ashleystahl/2015/11/06/how-to-land-a-job-in-90-seconds/?sh=53f6aa124802

Ok, you now have an appointment for an interview. You may be freaking out a little bit. You may be experiencing feelings of self-doubt. You may be asking yourself, "Do I Suck"? Relax, I've got you covered in this chapter. In this chapter we are going to do more of a deep dive into the job interview to help you present yourself like a Rock Star.

You probably don't want to show up at job interview looking like these Rock Stars.

You must keep in mind that an employer is NOT INTERESTED in your personal "self expression". They want to know how you will represent "their company" and "their brand". Armed with just this one piece of information, you can present yourself in a completely different way than 90% of the other applicants for any job!

Ask in the interview, "How can I best represent YOUR COMPANY?"

So let's dive into this!

When does the "interview" begin? It begins the first time you get a chance to present yourself to your potential employer.

Before the interview there may have been an application or resume you turned in or a phone call you had to set up the appointment. It's not uncommon at all to be introduced to a potential employer at an outside event or location. What kind of FIRST IMPRESSION are you giving people?

From thee two pictures, which first impression do you think is best for a potential employer to see?

The tricky thing is that you are ALWAYS giving others an opportunity to "interpret" you. Now I'm all about you having the freedom of self expression. There was a season in my life where I was all up in it – long ponytail, dangly earring, goatee, I was the bomb!! But take that "self expression" and put it into teaching elementary students in a small christian school and what do you think it got me???? FIRED!! Ha! For some reason, they just didn't seem to have an opening available the following year! They were not interested in my SELF EXPRESSION, they were looking for someone that could represent their company and their brand.

SO, WHEN DO YOU HAVE THIS OPPORTUNITY TO SHOW A POTENTIAL EMPLOYER THAT YOU CAN REPRESENT THEIR COMPANY BRAND?

» At school with your teachers, professors and coaches – they are people with jobs!

» At church around people with jobs (people that will be hiring you!)

» When you go out to dinner with your parents friends who are people with jobs

» When you are introduced to people with jobs

» Be aware of your social media – it's a big thing now!

» When you go to a community event and interact with people with jobs

» Your handwriting when you fill out an application that will go to people with jobs

» In short, whenever you go out of the house and you know you are going to be around people that have jobs!!!

ALL THESE PEOPLE ARE POTENTIAL "DOOR KEEPERS" FOR YOUR FUTURE!! HOW DO YOU SPEAK TO THEM? HOW DO YOU REPRESENT YOURSELF AROUND THEM?

Here are classic MUST DO'S when it comes to interacting with adults who have jobs:

» Establish solid eye contact.

» Smile when greeting someone.

» Say the other person's name when greeting them.

» Greet people with a firm handshake.

Boom! You have just outdone 80% of the other humans around you! These four steps – we'll call, "The Quad", will open doors for you that get closed for other people.

THE FIRST IMPRESSION DOESN'T JUST START AT THE INTERVIEW!!!

"67% of bosses say that failure to make eye contact is a common nonverbal mistake."

UNDERCOVER RECRUITER
HTTPS://THEUNDERCOVERRECRUITER.COM/INFOGRAPHIC-HOW-
INTERVIEWERS-KNOW-WHEN-HIRE-YOU-90-SECONDS/

> "When meeting new people, 55% of the impact comes from the way the person dresses, acts and walks through the door."

UNDERCOVER RECRUITER
HTTPS://THEUNDERCOVERRECRUITER.COM/INFOGRAPHIC-HOW-
INTERVIEWERS-KNOW-WHEN-HIRE-YOU-90-SECONDS/

Before the interview, when you interact with the company, be sure to find out the name of the person you are speaking with. If they are older than you and they give you their last name, refer to them as Mr. or Ms _____. If they don't give you their last name, just use the name they give you. Then when talking with them, use their name at least three times! People love to hear their name!!

At the interview, be sure to dress appropriately. Believe it or not, the interviewer will make very important decisions about you in the first 20 seconds. So, how can we make sure those decisions are favorable from the beginning and throughout the interview?

> » **Be on time** – Arrive 15 minutes early.
>
> » **Dress Appropriately** – Consider asking what the office dress code is and then plan on wearing something a little better.
>
> » **Body Language** – Look comfortable, but not too relaxed. Be natural in your posture. Avoid crossing your arms. I encourage people to sit on the edge of their seat and lean slightly forward in an interview.
>
> » **Be Prepared** – Have a general understanding of the company's purpose, core values and history. Be prepared to tell stories of how you have lived out these core values.

> » **Be Energetic** – You have to have positive energy that will contribute to an energetic workforce.
>
> » **Your Qualifications** – Looking good and talking good are great, but can you actually DO THE JOB? You'll need to be able to communicate your skills and desires.

While in the interview, a great way to set yourself apart from 90% of your competition is to ask questions. And this doesn't mean asking, "How much does it pay?" Remember, the company is hiring because they need a strong, willing workforce to do the work! You can present yourself as a great candidate by asking some of the following questions:

> » What does the perfect candidate for this job look like?
>
> » As a manager, what is your biggest frustration with your employees?
>
> » What is one thing you wish your employees would do on a consistent basis?
>
> » What is a problem you're trying to solve right now that you need the help of your employees to solve?

By asking these questions, you are identifying their need and revealing their pain! THEN YOU GET TO PROVIDE THE SOLUTION…YOU!!

Final thing on the interview… ASK FOR THE JOB!! No one does this! Actually say this, "How soon are you looking to fix this problem? If you'll hire

> "65% of bosses indicate that clothes could be a deciding factor between two almost identical candidates."
>
> **UNDERCOVER RECRUITER**
> HTTPS://THEUNDERCOVERRECRUITER.COM/INFOGRAPHIC-HOW-
> INTERVIEWERS-KNOW-WHEN-HIRE-YOU-90-SECONDS/

me, I can be here tomorrow and we can start fixing things immediately. Will you hire me?”

I know this sounds forward, but it's a huge differentiator for you! Ask for the job!!

"You have not because you ask not."

JAMES 4:2 NIV

After the interview, you need to follow up. No other candidate will do this! This comes across as extremely professional and organized.

Here are some follow up ideas for you.

1. Email the person that interviewed you within 3 hours of the interview thanking them for their time and including several more written references (not just names and contact info, but actual written references).

2. Send a thank you card within 24 hours.

3. If you know of another employee at the company, tell them that you had the interview and you would appreciate them giving you a good word "from the inside".

4. If you know of a person that has influence with the company, ask them to make a phone call on your behalf.

5. Be proactive!! It's not over at the interview!

....

"The number one most common mistake at a job interview is failing to ask for the job."

UNDERCOVER RECRUITER

HTTPS://THEUNDERCOVERRECRUITER.COM/INFOGRAPHIC-HOW-
INTERVIEWERS-KNOW-WHEN-HIRE-YOU-90-SECONDS/

References!

Have you ever had an influential person with a job give you a compliment? Have you ever had an employer say good things about you? Try this, the next time you get a compliment on your attitude or work ethic or production, ask the person, "May I quote you on that?"

I do this all the time with my company. It's a great way to capture references as you go. It can be tough waiting for people to get back with you on a written reference so just grab it when they say it! Then when you reference them, use their name, their job title and their company. This way you can generate dozens of references that can be used to overwhelm employers with your quality. You can also periodically post these references on your social media to get the word out that you are a High Quality Person and you don't suck.

Finally, there's something I've done a couple times for people and they ended up getting the job they wanted. If you know of an adult with a job that is willing to give you a good reference… GET IT ON VIDEO!!! Just use your phone and capture a quick 45 second video of them talking to a person that may be interested in hiring you. This can be generic. A written reference is nice, but video is MUCH BETTER! This makes for great follow up material!

Not everyone had great role models so let me be the one to tell you. These matter!

» The way you look

» Iron your clothes, everyday, be different, and take it up a notch

» The way you smell

» Don't smell like hell and don't put on too much perfume or cologne.

» The way you sound

» Be self-aware. Do you make noises when you concentrate? Are you a mouth breather? If yes, be aware and don't do it in an interview.

» The way you feel - you must learn how to step up and play the part of an A-Player, even when you don't feel like it. In sports, we call that putting on your game face.

Thoughts From Shawn

Back in Chapter One I talked about the experience I had interviewing for the position I have today. The moves that got me noticed are not rocket science, folks.

Back in Chapter One I talked about the experience I had interviewing for the position I have today. The moves that got me noticed are not rocket science, folks.

» I dressed for the job I wanted and not the job being offered (I dressed to impress).

» I showed up early.

» I sat up front.

» I stood up to present myself to the group rather than sitting.

» I made it a point to prepare and ask thoughtful questions.

» I followed the instructions in the invitation to the interview by bringing a copy of my resume.

» I insisted on getting the contact information of the interviewer to thank them and to send references.

I cannot stress enough that the moves in this chapter are FAR more than enough to set you apart from the VAST majority of people, regardless of the job you might be applying for. The question is: Now that you know them all, will you implement them? Remember the words of the late, great Chet Holmes, one of the world's best business coaches, and the former business partner of the billionaire Charlie Munger who said, "We all get good ideas at seminars and from books, radio talk shows and business-building gurus. However, implementation, not ideas, is the key to real success."

SHAWN LOWMAN

"JUST DON'T SUCK"

CHAPTER 6

HOW TO SET YOURSELF APART FROM THOSE THAT SUCK

"I know he can get the job, but can he DO the job?"

MR. WATURI
(*from the movie Joe Versus The Volcano*)

A-PLAYERS GET
THE JOB DONE...
PERIOD!

Now that you have made it through all the steps and you have actually gotten the job, how do you set yourself apart from other employees who are in competition for raises and promotions.

As a business owner since 2012 and as a business consultant who has worked with hundreds of business owners and managers, I have a unique insight on the essentials needed for you to get noticed and rewarded. It really comes down to just two main things - Work Ethic and Talent.

Here are some very encouraging stats for you to consider:

It cost 1.7x more to hire outside than to hire internally.

https://www.forbes.com/sites/danschawbel/2013/10/21/the-top-10-work-place-trends-of-2013/#6eba79007c42

40% external hires don't work out vs. 25% of internal hires not working out Society of Human Resource Managers

https://www.shrm.org/hr-today/news/hr-magazine/pages/010215-hiring.aspx

The reason why I'm sharing these stats with you is because, once you're in the company, you can tap into these paths of promotion easier than an outsider.

So let's take a look at these two essential characteristics needed to get noticed and rewarded.

Dictionary.com defines talent as a special ability that allows you to do something well. A skill that you have mastered as a result of diligent practice.

There's a difference between Talent and Gift!

I love the second part of the definition of talent - a skill you have mastered as a result of diligent practice. Oh, that's good! This was one of the key problems that I discovered in myself when I entered the workplace. I had some gifts, but I lacked talent; skills developed through diligent practice. I had some wonderful God-given gifts that I relied on. I used those gifts to find a measure of success in things that I was a part of throughout my life in school. However, in so many areas, I didn't put in the time and discipline needed to really develop these gifts into true talents. As a result, I was limited in my ability to provide greater and greater value in the workplace. It's your responsibility to turn your gifts into talents.

GIFT	TALENT
Free	Cost
Easy	Hard
Immediate	Takes Time
Given	Developed
A Mustard Seed	A Large Tree
	Providing Shelter

"Growth mindset says that your basic gifts can be developed into greater talent. This is in contrast to a "Fixed Mindset".

CAROL DWECK
(World-renowned Stanford University professor and author of best selling "Mindsets")

"I don't divide the world into the weak and the strong, or the successes and the failures... I divide the world into learners and non-learners."

BENJAMIN BARBER
(Eminent Sociologist)

So, what does that mean when you are faced with a difficult situation? Will you learn and grow or will you stay and gripe? When faced with a situation that required more out of me than my "gift" provided, I would get mad and start complaining. This pouting kept me constantly focused on my "gift" and neglecting the need to turn that gift into a talent.

MORE TALENT, MORE VALUE!

Some talents I've had to learn starting at age 47 when I started my company include:

- MANAGEMENT
- SALES
- MARKETING
- EMPLOYEE MANAGEMENT
- BUSINESS LEADERSHIP
- SPEAKING
- SEARCH ENGINE OPTIMIZATION
- NETWORKING
- INSPIRING EMPLOYEES
- COACHING/TEACHING
- WRITING
- EDITING

All of these have gone into my talent bank that continues to expand! Gifts are limited but talents never stop growing if you stay at it.

I've grown in these talents and it's increased my ability to make more and more money as a result.

What is the hole in the company where you work? Where does your boss (owner) think the business needs to grow and improve? What are the goals for this year? What activities need to be added, expanded or deleted from the daily schedule to help the business meet these goals?

This is your opportunity! Now, what talent do you need to grow in to help fill that hole!! Commit to mastering that talent that fills the hole!!

Some people (not you) would say, "But Clay, I don't have any talents."

I stumbled on a Google graphic one time that listed the 10 things that require zero talent:

- BEING ON TIME
- A STRONG WORK ETHIC
- EFFORT
- BODY LANGUAGE
- ENERGY
- ATTITUDE
- PASSION
- BEING TEACHABLE
- DOING EXTRA
- BEING PREPARED

If you want to get paid well you must always obsessively be thinking about how you can use your talents to make the company more money, decrease costs for the company, or help the company save time.

The second key quality you will need to get noticed and rewarded is Work Ethic. Dictionary.com defines work ethic as a belief in the moral benefit and importance of work and its inherent ability to strengthen character.

"Never let anyone outwork you or out hussle you. Ever."

RICK PITTINO - COLLEGE BASKETBALL COACH

"The only thing that I see that is distinctly different about me is I'm not afraid to die on a treadmill. I will not be out-worked, period. You might have more talent than me, you might be smarter than me, you might be sexier than me, you might be all of those things. You may have me in nine categories, but if we get on the treadmill together, there's two things: You're getting off first, or I'm going to die. It's really that simple, right?

You're not going to out-work me. It's such a simple, basic concept. The guy who is willing to hustle the most is going to be the guy that just gets that loose ball. The majority of people who aren't getting the places they want or aren't achieving the things that they want in this business is strictly based on hustle. It's strictly based on being out-worked; it's strictly based on missing crucial opportunities. I say all the time if you stay ready, you ain't gotta get ready."

WILL SMITH

Nominated for five Golden Globe Awards and two Academy Awards, and has won four Grammy Awards

Clay's Staires Steps To Becoming Irreplaceable At Your Work...

- » **Be the Spark**
- » **Spread the Fire**

Be the Spark

Ask your boss, manager, or direct report these questions.

- » Where does our company have a hole?

- » What is the talent gap?

- » What talent do I need to master to fill this gap?

The boss saves money by not hiring from the outside. 70% of the cost is saved by promoting great people like you from within the company.

"Do not let your fire go out, spark by irreplaceable spark in the hopeless swamps of the not-quite, the not-yet, and the not-at-all. Do not let the hero in your soul perish in lonely frustration for the life you deserved and have never been able to reach. The world you desire can be won. It exists.. it is real.. it is possible.. it's yours."

AYN RAND
(Author of two bestselling books;
The Fountainhead and Atlas Shrugged)

Is there a position in your company that you want to be in? You have to appoint yourself to that position. Don't wait for someone to appoint you! As much as you can, step into that position. Without overstepping, begin daily fulfilling some of the responsibilities of that position.

- » Do you need to come to work earlier or stay later? Do it.

- » Do you need to dress differently? Do it, if you can.

- » Do you need to help others more? Do it.

- » Do you need to sell more? Do it.

- » Do you need to clean more? Do it.

- » Do you need to be more willing to do whatever needs to be done? Do it.

- » Do you need to stop complaining and keep others from complaining? Do it.

Whatever is needed in that new position… Do it! Be the problem fixer not the problem maker or just the problem identifier.

Once you begin solving problems, don't parade around advertising all the extra work you're doing. No one likes that person. Just do it and move on looking for the next problem to solve. Stop being a problem or being a part of the problem. Be the solution. If you don't know what the problem is, remember to ask your boss about what problems they are trying to solve.

Be the example of the, "I can fix this problem" employee.

Thomas Edison once wrote,

"Success is 99% perspiration and 1% inspiration".

You get the idea? The inspiration is the Spark!

DISCLAIMER - Do NOT go up to your boss tomorrow and tell them all the problems YOU SEE at your company. This will just piss them off. It's easy to see problems. True A-Players, who don't suck, solve problems, they don't create them. Ask your boss what problems they see. Over time you can actually learn to see what your boss sees. I call this the Shepherd's Eye. Wow! An employee that can actually see what the boss sees and has an ability to solve problems in the business is incredibly valuable to a boss or business owner. Be that person.

Spread the Fire

Jack Welch, the former CEO of General Electric who increased the value of the company by 4000% during his tenure explained the 4E's that he was looking for when hiring:

- » Energy
- » Energize
- » Execute
- » Edge

Principle - You gotta bring the fire to the job! According to Inc.com, 78% of workers are checked out during the workday! Almost 8 out of 10. Again, Just Don't Suck! Only 2 employees out of 10 are engaged at work. Be that employee. If you don't want to be that employee, then you probably suck. This doesn't mean you're a bad person, you're just a bad employee.

Spark is the energy you bring each day. Spreading the fire is about being the Energizer in your company. A company that is growing is a company where the fire has spread! Look for holes in the company and then take your spark to it.

Be contagious, not obnoxious.

Remember this from chapter 1? I asked 30+ business owners what they look for in their employees. This is a summary of what they said.

☐ Dependable	☐ Coachable
☐ Honest	☐ Growth mindset
☐ Consistent Positive Attitude	☐ Reliable
☐ Ability to communicate well	☐ Good work ethic
☐ A good appearance	☐ Always on time
☐ A good work history	☐ Energetic
☐ Self-motivated	☐ Adaptable

You must commit to being all in for 18-24 months! This is how long it will take to get you firmly on the path to where you want to go.

- » Change Your Reputation - 2-3 months

- » Change the Conversation - 2-3 months

- » Change Your Compensation - 6 months

- » Change Your Practical Education - 12 months

Say to yourself over and over, "I'm not stopping until I get there!"

At this "Worker Level" in the company you work for, it's not about "your" ideas, it's about "your" ability to consistently produce results in the daily, repetitive responsibilities you have. Most of life is a repetitive grind. This is where most people fail. They are always looking for something new; something fresh and different. It's true for the workplace as well as in relationships, entertainment, recreation… in just about everything. It's like we have a defect in the human condition that makes us susceptible to distraction and attention deficit. But those that can stay focused and develop the ability and tenacity to win at this level will come out with the mindset necessary to win on the battleground called the marketplace.

CHAPTER 7
EMPLOYEE EVALUATIONS

YOU MUST INSPECT WHAT YOU EXPECT.

Being a school teacher for 15 years gave me that chance to write a ton of examinations. When creating a test for my students, I would look through the material and make decisions on questions based on what concepts I felt were most important for them to know. It's the same for employee evaluations that are designed to measure the most important aspects of your job.

The evaluation is THE document you want to look at to discover what is important to your manager.

Remember how nice it was when the teacher in school would hand out the Study Guide for the test? I remember Mr. Sheehan doing this in eleventh grade science and then all the questions on the test would be from the study guide! It took all the guesswork out of it. I literally knew what was going to be on the test so I knew what to study and focus on. Your Employee Evaluation is just the same. See if you can get a copy of a blank evaluation form so you can know what to stay focused on each day in your job.

Being a Great Employee is not rocket science! It's not some secret that only a few people know. The question is, "Are you willing to do what's needed to be a great employee?"

Take a moment to write down some qualities that you think are important for a Great Employee to have? You can refer back to the description of A, B and C Players if you want. Also, if you're not sure about these qualities, ASK YOUR MANAGER!! No one does this and it's another move to set you apart from everyone else.

How can you practically walk out each of the company values each day in your job? Here's a detailed script that you can actually use to help you with the conversation with your manager.

> » " (Your managers name) , what are the top three qualities you look for in a great employee here at (company name)?"
>
>> > They will answer you.
>
> » "Ok, that's very helpful. What specifically can I do better?

Boom! That's it! But no one does this because most employees suck! But not you because you're reading this book.

Many times, just like in school, evaluations aren't so much a test of an employees knowledge and skill as much as it is about an employee's CHARACTER or their attitude.

There are four main categories that employers will evaluate in their employees:

> » **Your Knowledge** - what you know and how quickly you learn something.
>
> » **Your Skill** - what you can do and how quickly you can pick up something.

» **Character** - who you are

» **Production** - what you can get done for the company

When I train managers, I teach them to evaluate their employees constantly. You see, an evaluation isn't just AN EVENT. An evaluation is an ongoing, day by day, measurement of how much value an employee is adding to the company. Unfortunately, many managers only do evaluations once a year or once a quarter. This leaves far too much time passing before giving constructive feedback to members of the team. Obviously, this is far too long.

As mentioned in the last chapter, Jack Welch, (a good name for you to know) the former CEO of General Electric that grew his companies revenues over 4000% while he was the CEO, created a system that allowed him to constantly evaluate his employees. This is a great scorecard you should keep in mind each day. He called it The 4 E's:

Energy

How much personal energy an employee puts into their work?

Energize

Does the employee have the ability to pass on their positive energy to other employees (inspire)?

Execution

Does the employee have the skills and ability to do the work they have been hired to do?

Edge

Does the employee have the ability to work through difficulty (to do what has to be done)?

 Jack Welch used these four categories and he would give his employees a "grade" – A to C. He could do this each day, in a short amount of time and for multiple employees to help them know how they were doing. If you scored a C in Execution, you knew exactly where you needed to improve.

My point is that evaluations are imperative to ensure quality production and performance. If managers don't evaluate their people then they are doomed to have to tolerate low level employees - C Players. Evaluations are YOUR FRIEND!

We have come to associate "evaluations" with very negative emotions. I remember thinking like this. I was scared of evaluations (tests) because I was afraid I would fail! The great thing about employee evaluations is you can actually DECIDE to pass with flying colors and actually do it! Remember to ask your manager for a copy of the evaluation form ahead of time so you can know what you will be evaluated on. Get the answers to the test! Just like the study guide in school.

HOW TO ROCK AN
EMPLOYEE EVALUATION:

RESPECT – This is a character issue. Treat your co-employees, manager and customers with respect. You don't have to "like" them, but you must respect them and the role they play in the company. If you can't respect them, don't stay around and be a sucking consumer. Man up (or… woman up?) and go get another job.

OVERDELIVER – Learn what is on the evaluation and be determined to go above and beyond to set yourself apart from the status quo. It's not hard! Remember 8 out of 10 workers are disengaged!! One easy way to over deliver is to show up early and stay late. In today's marketplace, it's not extremely difficult to stand out of the crowd. Overdeliver for 8 to 10 months, after that, if nobody recognizes it or rewards it, it's time to look for a new job.

COMMITMENT – This is huge! Understand, it's not commitment to yourself, but it's commitment to the vision and mission of the company. If you truly want to be a great leader, you must learn how to be a servant first. Will you "commit" to this process of learning how to be a STAR employee? You gotta do this for 8-10 months at least before you can expect any recognition or reward.

KNOWLEDGE – Be quick to pick up new knowledge and understanding in your job. Seek out information that will allow you to be remarkable in your position. Become the employee that inspires people to want to know more about the company and its products and services. You must do this for, at least, 8-10 months. If you stop for a week and go back to being a B-Player, the clock starts all over again. BE CONSISTENT!!

A-PLAYERS EMBRACE EVALUATIONS BECAUSE:

» #1 – They love to win.

» #2 – They're not afraid! They know they have been meeting (and exceeding expectations) because of the constant positive feedback they have been getting.

» #3 – They thrive in a learning and growing environment.

» #4 - They know that evaluations and consequences will weed out the poor performers that are frustrating them and making the team look bad.

When was your last evaluation? How did you do? If you didn't score as well as you wanted, how did you respond? Your response to the evaluation is as important as the evaluation itself.

DON'T GET BITTER, GET BETTER!

So, when is your next evaluation? What can you begin doing immediately to ensure that you ROCK it? List 3 action steps you know you need to take to dominate your evaluation.

"JUST DON'T SUCK"

CHAPTER 8
GETTING NOTICED AND GETTING PROMOTED

"You can have everything you want in life, if you just help enough other people get what they want."

ZIG ZIGLAR
(THE LEGENDARY BEST-SELLING AUTHOR AND SELF HELP EXPERT)

Not too long ago I read a book called The Gospel of Wealth by Andrew Carnegie. Carnegie was the King of Steel in the 19th century. In the introduction to the book, pages 4-10, Carnegie describes the story of how he became the wealthiest man in America in his time. The reason why I bring it up in this book is because it contains 8 Steps that he intentionally took to obtain his success. Keep in mind that it's the combination of ALL EIGHT STEPS that makes this work. Not completing all 8 may easily leave you short and offended that they didn't work for you... but you have to do them all! Remember, it takes time to do them all and this is where most people (that suck) check out. Delayed gratification isn't in the C-Players vocabulary.

I'm sure that young Carnegie didn't fully understand that he was working his way through these steps while he was in the midst of it. He just didn't quit, and over time he discovered that the path is very similar for every successful person. Not fully seeing the path is actually part of the process. If it was easily seen, many more people would do it. Success requires a measure of faith. Without it, you'll give up at some point along the difficult journey.

So, let's take a look at these 8 Steps To Success that Andrew Carnegie left behind for us like bread crumbs.

STEP #1 - Escape The Wolf of Poverty - Set your mind and your full energy on the goal of being successful.

Carnegie describes his "first serious lesson of his life" when he and his father had taken the last of their goods to the merchant and returned to their home greatly distressed because there was no more work to be found. He learned from a very early age that as long as you work for someone else, you give up the power to create money at will.

STEP #2 - Work hard and appreciate your work - Carnegie worked six days a week in his first job at the age of just 12 years old as a "bobbin-boy" in a cotton factory. He was paid $1.20 a week.

"I cannot tell you how proud I was when I received my first week's earnings. One dollar and twenty cents made by myself and given to me because I had been of some use in the world. No longer entirely dependent upon my parents, but at last admitted to the family partnership as a contributing member and able to help them! It is everything to feel that you are useful."

Have you experienced this gratitude with your paycheck recently? Is this a common emotion for you or have you been pulled into the Valley Of Those That Suck and complain about your wages and blame your boss because they aren't paying you enough all while standing there without the guts to go make your life and stop waiting for someone to hand it to you. Gratitude is essential to becoming successful. It is the attitude that attracts the great unseen hand of opportunity to your doorstep.

STEP #3 - Be willing to go backward to go forward.

He was grateful but he "knew from within that this would not, could not, should not last - I should someday get into a better position."

There was a Scotsman who owned another factory and he noticed young Andrew and took him into his factory before he turned 13. At the beginning it was worse than the cotton factory because he had to manage a boiler in the basement and run the steam engine which drove the machinery.

The responsibility of keeping all the machinery going and not blowing up the factory was a great strain and it led to nightmares. "But I never told them at home that I was having a hard time. No, no! Everything must be bright to them."

Everyone in the family was working. There was a culture of doing good work. "No man would whine or complain - he would die first."

STEP #4 - Stand out - Do something better than everyone else.

The Scottish factory owner discovered that young Andrew could "write and cipher (do math)" so he soon took him out of the basement because they needed someone to "make out the bills and keep their accounts". But he still had to do all of the boiler work as well because the clerking just took a little bit of time.

STEP #5 - Keep moving forward and don't get stuck in a comfortable compromise.

Using his experience as a clerk, young Andrew was able to secure a job as a messenger boy in a telegraph office in Pittsburgh at the age of 14. His responsibility was to deliver messages to six different newspaper offices all over the city. Unfortunately, he didn't know the city very well. "However, I made up my mind that I would learn to repeat successfully each business house in the city and was soon able to shut my eyes and envision each firm by name." He was determined to conquer any obstacle that got in his way. He kept moving forward and didn't see difficulties as boundaries.

His new goal was to become a manager over the messenger boys. He began arriving early to work to practice the skills needed for this position. One morning, upon receiving a telegraph message, he decided to take the message to one of the newspaper offices himself before being told by a manager. He took a risk and it paid off. Soon other managers were asking him to work for them.

Soon he began to take the telegraph messages by ear; a skill that only two people had in the entire country. This skill brought him a lot of attention and he was soon promoted to become a manager and his pay was increased to $25/month - $300 a year! (that's just under $10,000 in 2020 money) This was the exact amount that he had set as a goal back when he was in the factory because this was the amount of money that his family could live on each year and be quite comfortable.

STEP #6 - Create multiple active streams of revenue.

Use your gifts and talents beyond your job. Each of the six newspaper offices in Pittsburgh relied on receiving telegrams from the central offices. One person in the central office had the job of collecting the telegraphs and delegating them out to messengers to take to each of the six papers. This "deliverer" received $6 a week for the work. Seeing Carnegie's ambition, the man in this delivery position offered a gold dollar every week if young Andrew would take over that job. He accepted it and soon every reporter was coming to him each evening for the news that he had for them. This brought him into contact with men that could open doors to his future. "I think this step of doing something beyond one's job is fully entitled to be considered 'business'." The other salary was in exchange for regular work, but this extra dollar a week was different. This dollar represented a little business operation that gave him revenue beyond what he needed to survive.

STEP #7 - Make Connections with influential Gatekeepers.

In time, the Pennsylvania Railroad completed tracks to Pittsburgh. The superintendent of the railway was Thomas A. Scott and he often came to the telegraph office to talk to it's chief. It was during one of these visits that young Andrew was able to meet Mr. Scott. When the railway system put up its own wiring for telegraphs, Scott asked Carnegie to be his clerk and manager. So he left the telegraph office (he kept moving forward) and became connected to the railway. This new position increased his income to $35 a month. When Carnegie discovered that Mr. Scott was making $125 a month, he set a new goal to match it!

STEP #8 - Find a Mentor - Mentors hold the keys to your potential.

Carnegie remained with the Pennsylvania Railway for 13 years and became the successor of Mr. Scott as he had risen to the office of the vice president of the company. Now he was making $125 a month. Mr. Scott had taken quite a liking to young Andrew and spent time with him teaching him how to be successful.

These moves are still the moves today, almost 200 years later. Where are you along this path? If it were a checklist, what could you check off?

- ☐ Escape The Wolf of Poverty
- ☐ Work hard and appreciate your work
- ☐ Be willing to go backward to go forward
- ☐ Stand out
- ☐ Find a mentor
- ☐ Keep moving forward and don't get stuck in a comfortable compromise
- ☐ Create multiple active streams of revenue
- ☐ Make connections with influential gatekeepers

It took me until age 50 to master Step 1. I had mastered steps 2, 3, 4, and 5 but I didn't even know that I had to escape The Wolf of Poverty. My mentor (#8), Clay Clark, taught me how to do this. Keep in mind that it's not just a linear path. Once you get to #8, you haven't all of a sudden "arrived". This will be an expanding journey through the rest of your life as you move from season to season.

Which of these steps do you need to work on to help you move forward? What do you think completing this step will look like? If you are stuck, who will be your Clay Clark? Who will be your mentor to push you past where you currently find yourself stuck?

Thoughts From Shawn

This stuff is just as simple as the guidelines outlined in Chapter 5. I have two specific and very implementable moves for you. These steps may be simple but they are by no means easy.

Move 1: Beat your boss to work every day. There is nothing more immediately noticeable to a manager or owner and almost nobody is willing to do it consistently.

Move 2: Over-deliver. Whatever the task may be you need to produce a better result than your co-workers OR produce a faster result than your co-workers OR do more of the task than your co-workers. This is the fastest way to increase your value to the organization and get considered for promotion.

SHAWN LOWMAN

CHAPTER 9
FINDING THE RIGHT JOB FOR YOU

When you are young and without a lot of work experience, it's very difficult to find "the right job". It takes time, trying several different positions in different companies to discover what you really like doing, what kind of environment you enjoy working in, what you're really good at, and what you really suck at. I'm a big fan of having multiple experiences in the workforce to help you learn who you are in the marketplace and what you're passionate about bringing to the marketplace. I'm sure you've heard the phrase, "Find something you love to do and you'll never have to work a day in your life."

Well, that's a nice phrase, but it's very misleading. Yes, you want to find something you enjoy doing, but if "enjoying the work" is the main goal of your work, you're in for a very disappointing career in the marketplace, especially for your first 15 to 20 years. It takes this amount of time to grind it out and grow your character and your skills. It takes time to stick with a job to master the skills needed to really enjoy the work.

Bestselling author, Robert Green, in his book, *Mastery*, explains the four phases of the development of a master craftsman in any area of life. He maps out the historically proven path that many, many masters went through to reach their ultimate achievements. Leonardo Da Vinci, Mozart, Thomas Edison, Charles Darwin, Martha

Graham and many others were able to achieve a level of mastery that they were able to live in on a daily basis. The point is, personal development takes time. It's a journey not a destination.

Malcolm Gladwell, in his bestselling book *Outliers: The Story of Success*, popularized a common rule of thumb, "It takes 10,000 hours of 'deliberate practice' to become world-class in any field". Now, does it really take 10,000 hours exactly? I'm not going to debate the exact number, but the nature of the idea is that it takes time to  get really good at something and until you're really good at it, it's probably not going to be a lot of fun! Ask anyone in their fourth month of piano lessons if it's fun. Ask anyone in their first weeks of running if it's fun. Ask anyone in their first 3 years of owning a business if it's fun. Each of these people will answer a resounding, "NO!"

I remember taking guitar lessons and the strings killing my fingers until I developed callouses. It wasn't fun and I didn't "enjoy" it.

I remember taking Spanish lessons and getting all the nouns and verbs and tenses all mixed up. It was so frustrating and I didn't enjoy it.

I remember spending extra hours shooting free-throws so I wouldn't let the team down. I didn't enjoy it, but it was that extra time that made me confident to go to the line - and I did it a lot.

I remember first starting out as a high school teacher and learning how to teach other people what I knew and learning how to inspire and train rather than just teach a subject. It was hard and the students let me know that I sucked at it everyday. I didn't enjoy it. But sticking with it and grinding it out over time is what helped me be voted by the student body as Teacher of the Year in my TENTH YEAR OF TEACHING! Let's do some math here…

6 hours of teaching each day for 180 days a year for 10 years equals… wait for it… 10,800 hours of teaching! Wow! The rule of thumb is proven. Boom!

Most employees suck because they haven't taken the time to get better. It takes time to get good at something and most people are unwilling to put in the time to learn. Most people see a job title and envision themselves "loving it". Then they get the job and for the first two weeks it may be great, but the "loving it" quickly fades in the midst of the mundane every-day-ness of it. Now, because it isn't fun and they don't really enjoy it, they begin to disengage and do as little as possible because the only thing they do enjoy is getting a paycheck but even that soon fades and they move on to another job without learning what is necessary to learn in your work.

So this chapter is about what you need to learn at your jobs so you can have a greater and greater confidence in choosing the best job for you so you don't end up like 68% of American Workers that are DISENGAGED at work according to a 2018 Gallup poll.

https://www.inc.com/sonia-thompson/68-percent-of-employees-are-disen-gaged-but-there-i.html

Now that we understand that it will take time to discover what you like and what you don't like and to learn the skills necessary to actually enjoy the work, it's very important for you to learn your personal Core Values and your purpose for working in the first place. At some point in your career, your purpose must go beyond just getting a paycheck to pay for your life. All "A-Player Employees" and successful people have been able to connect their purpose for work to some greater good. It's that purpose that will give your work meaning. Without it, even though you may be really good at a job, you will be constantly frustrated without feeling any level of fulfillment from your work.

Have you ever considered what your 5-7 Core Values are in your life? Have you ever thought about what your mission in life is or what you were put on this planet to achieve? These are deep questions that every employee that doesn't suck has spent time answering to some level.

Take a moment to write down your Core Values:

What are your personal Core Values?

These are fundamental beliefs that you have that make up the foundation of how you view life and work.

_____

_____

_____

WHAT IS YOUR LIFE VISION?

This can be tough to clarify and articulate when you're young. Your life vision is a picture of what you were put on earth to create? For me, now that I have over 50 years to look back on, I can say that my life vision is, "To set people free." It's that simple. But it took 50 years to find that simplicity.

_____

_____

_____

WHAT IS YOUR LIFE MISSION?

Your life mission is simply a description of the "vehicle" you will use to fulfill your vision. For instance, my life vision is to set people free. The vehicle I use to do this is teaching, coaching, inspiring, and mentoring. I did this as a high school science teacher for 15 years, as a minister for 10 years, as a business owner for 10 years and my next step is to do it as a politician.

_____

_____

_____

WHAT TYPE OF CULTURE DO YOU THRIVE IN?

This is simply the type of environment that you feel is most conducive to functioning at your best and highest.

_____

_____

_____

Once you have an idea of your personal core values and mission in life, it's important for you to consider the Core Values of any company where you would like to work. Do you now know what they are? Do you know the "Vision" of the company? Why did the owner start the company? How did they see their vision being "walked out" to the town/city/state/country/world on a daily basis? What did they dream would be the daily "atmosphere" in the business (the work environment)?

Your very first step in determining if a "job" is right for you, is to confirm that YOU ALIGN WITH THE COMPANY! In other words, before you look at the Job, look at the Company.

Let's take a look at some other company core values.

All Employees

Live the Southwest Way

Warrior Spirit
Strive to be the best
Display a sense of urgency
Never give up

Servant's Heart
Follow The Golden Rule
Treat others with respect
Embrace our Southwest Family

Fun-LUVing Attitude
Be a passionate Team Player
Don't take yourself too seriously
Celebrate successes

Work the Southwest Way

Work Safely
Follow standard operating procedures
Identify and report hazards
Respect and comply with regulations

Wow Our Customers
Deliver world-class Hospitality
Create memorable connections
Be famous for friendly service

Keep Costs Low
Show up and work hard
Protect our ProfitSharing
Find a better way

TOMS

While traveling in Argentina in 2006, TOMS Founder, Blake Mycoskie, witnessed the hardships faced by children growing up without shoes. Wanting to help, he created TOMS Shoes, a company that would match every pair of shoes purchased with a new pair of shoes for a child in need. One for One®.

» An entrepreneurial spirit

» Acting with integrity

» Respect for each other

» Giving back to the community

https://jobs.comcast.com

https://careers.heb.com/about-h-e-b/

Do you like the words used in these core values? Do these words "connect" with you? Do these "environments and values" sound like a place where you could grow and thrive? If so, then companies with these types of core values may be a good "fit" for you. If not, no matter what the "job" is, you won't find long term happiness in these companies.

It all begins with aligning YOUR Why with the COMPANY's Why.

So, now, on a scale from 1-10 (with 10 being the highest), how well do you feel like YOU align with the values of the company where you currently work? _____

Do you align? This is the great MISTAKE that so many people make when looking for work and accepting a position at a company. In their desire to get a "paycheck" they neglect to consider what it will be like to "live" in the environment each day. The check may be great, but if the values are different, you will soon find yourself feeling like they couldn't pay you enough to keep coming in every day and give 100% effort!

This is very likely a key ingredient in the fact that 68% of American Workers are DISENGAGED at work.

https://www.inc.com/sonia-thompson/68-percent-of-employees-are-disen-gaged-but-there-i.html

The RIGHT job isn't just the job that will give you the money you want!

When you are in an interview, it's important that you INTERVIEW THE COMPANY to discover what their values and culture are. Yes, you can go to a website and find their written values, but you'll want to ask the interviewer to give you an explanation for each one and what each one looks like on a daily basis in the workplace. If they say, "Yes, we have that." You want to respond with, "Cool, what does that look like each day in the office with clients and with customers?"

The job description will tell you what level of skill and knowledge you will need for the job. However, the interview should be designed to determine if you FIT in the company. Unfortunately the people getting interviewed and the one doing the interview don't understand this and so getting hired becomes all about, "Will you do the work" and "Will you give me money" and less about the Who and Why. Again, going into an interview knowing this about the interviewer and being armed with this information will cause you to STAND OUT among all the other candidates.

Ask yourself these questions before you interview:

» What is my personality?

» What kind of environment do I really enjoy being in?

» What kind of people do I enjoy spending time with?

» What kind of work do I enjoy doing for long periods of time?

**Then, in an interview, when they ask you, "Do you have any questions",
be prepared to ask...**

1. "Yes, tell me about your company's core values."

2. "When you think about your best employee, what characteristics come to your mind that make them stand out among all the others?"

3. "When you think about the perfect candidate to fill this position, what do you see?" (push for character quality answers and as well as "skill and ability" answers)

The answers they give you to each of these questions will give you insight into what they think are the most important qualities in their employees. Their answers should line up with their core values and support their culture. If you discover that their "perfect candidate description" does not align with who you are, then this position may not be the best FIT for you. If you take a job that is not a good fit for you or if you choose to take a job at a company that doesn't fit you, then don't be surprised if you aren't happy working there. It doesn't mean it was a bad decision, it just means that you won't ever find fulfillment at this job. There's no need to keep hanging around complaining, just start looking around for a better fit and learn from the experience.

Notice I didn't have any questions here about the actual WORK that you will be doing.

Disclaimer: When you're young and just entering into the workforce, you may not know the answers to a lot of these questions that I've asked you to ask of yourself. In most cases, it's important for you to get out there and work a number of jobs; doing a number of things in a number of different environments to really discover what's your best fit. You need to discover what you're good at, what you're great at and what you suck at.

I had breakfast one morning with Ian, a recent college graduate that was then looking for his first professional job. He asked me what he should look for when choosing a job. I started talking about what I thought would be the most important factors to consider. Below is the list that I created in response to his question.

Here are the 5 Areas of Development that you may want to consider as a young employee to determine if this job with this company is going to help you grow and prepare you for your NEXT job! Does this company intentionally help you in these 5 areas...

FIVE CORE AREAS OF PROFESSIONAL DEVELOPMENT

SKILL DEVELOPMENT

These are "hard job skills" that you'll use to get a job and do the job, as well as the "soft skills" like communication, problem solving and leadership. Will you actually learn important skills that will help you in the future?

MARKETPLACE POSITIONING

This is simply being positioned to be "hireable" by a larger company. Will this job get you in front of the right people who will then open doors for my future?

FINANCIAL SUSTAINABILITY

Does this company/job have the ability to pay you well enough to help you move forward? Are there opportunities to make more money if you don't suck? Is there any kind of financial training that comes with working at this company? It's one thing to make enough money today to pay your bills, but does this job provide you with a growing paycheck as you move into your future?

PERSONAL DEVELOPMENT

Does this job provide any kind of ongoing training or personal development workshops or opportunities? Are there mentorship programs available? Discovering your identity, your life purpose, your strengths and weaknesses.

SERVANT LEADERSHIP

A vital ingredient in discovering your place in the bigger picture of life is having opportunities to GIVE back to others. Too often we see the universe revolving around "us". To be great in life, you must learn how to be a servant and have compassion for others. Does this company provide opportunities for you to give of your time, talents and treasures to improve the lives of others?

THIS GIVES YOU MORE TO TALK ABOUT IN YOUR INTERVIEW WHEN THEY ASK YOU, "DO YOU HAVE ANY QUESTIONS?"

"JUST DON'T SUCK"

CHAPTER 10
WHY I WROTE THIS BOOK

I heard it in the distance and it was terrifying. It wasn't supposed to be there. This was supposed to be safe; just a fun day of adventure like so many others I had with Shawn, Larry Dale and Curtis at Seven Caves just a mile from my childhood home in northeastern Oklahoma. But that sound changed everything. The sound turned the adventure into survival. This was real!

This literally happened to me back in 1970 when I was in 6th grade. There was an old abandoned limestone quarry near my home that the locals called "Seven Caves". Dangerous as a copperhead, but a perfect adventureland for some country boys to explore. I spent a lot of time there as a kid playing in the caves, climbing the rock faces to the top and then sliding back down old, abandoned oil pipes into the quarry. Even the trail to get to the caves was filled with adventure and danger. It included having to traverse a two-hundred-foot train trestle (bridge). It looked similar to the train trestle in the movie Stand By Me but not quite as big or as high, but definitely high enough to peak the imagination of a young boy headed to some hidden caves plastered with "No Trespassing" signs.

The four of us had been to the caves many times, but on this day we had a new experience that none of us had planned on. As we walked across the trestle, we were almost to the middle when we heard the sound of "The Train!" It was just like in the movie; we were caught. The railroad ties were about six inches apart with nothing between them except for the nearly hundred-foot drop to the creek below. We all started screaming and trying to run. Have you ever tried to run fast when your stride is just six inches? Thinking back on it, I'm cracking up as I'm sitting here writing this, picturing what we must have looked like when we first started running before realizing we could take longer strides. All four of us were yelling and running to the end of the bridge. I just remember feeling so confused and conflicted between running or jumping as I sped along. Which was the best chance for survival? Larry and Curtis reached the end of the bridge first. As Shawn and I reached the end, I remember looking back and the train was still far away, but my heart was racing like I had just escaped certain death! I'll never forget that sound. Even now, over 40 years later, when I hear a train whistle, it takes me back to that sunny day in the heat of an Oklahoma summer at Seven Caves.

Unfortunately, that wasn't the last time I would hear "the train whistle of sudden change" in my life and be caught completely off guard. All the other times were more figurative, but they elicited the same panic and conflict of whether to run forward or to bail out. There was the time as I walked across the South Oval on the University of Oklahoma campus after taking the last final of my college career. That "train whistle" was the realization that I now had to go get a job and I wasn't ready. There was another "train whistle" on the first night of my honeymoon in my first marriage. That "whistle" created the same panicked feelings as I said to myself, "Oh, no. What have I done?" Then there was the "train whistle" that went off when I was 25 years old and heard my dad say, "Clay, you're fired". I had planned to spend my whole life working in my family's business and suddenly it was over. This again, brought about those feelings of panic and fear. There have been many more "train whistle" experiences in my life as reality crashed down on me like a sudden avalanche, completely catching me unaware and unprepared for what was ahead of me. And every time, it was accompanied by the fear and confusion associated with panic. Each time I said to myself, "I'm not ready for the next step!"

That's why I have written this book. My hope is that the practical tools in this book will equip you with the strength and confidence you need to outrun that train and get to safety on the other side of the bridge. I wish I had a road map like this when I was moving into all those seasons of transition so I could have a good look on the other side of the panic and be confidently prepared for the steps I needed to take when it came time to apply for a job, go to an interview, or to compete in the work force on a daily basis.

You see, I had many of the characteristics associated with people that "suck". I had all the characteristics that employees in this generation are accused of today. The difference between me and today's generation is simply a matter of access. I didn't have access to information and the opportunities that are available today. If I had, I would most likely have been very similar to the generation of today.

There just weren't the options that are available today. There weren't any stories of the 19-year-old millionaire. Fast riches in tech companies weren't around yet. There were no models of "living with parents until you were 30". There weren't video game communities to keep me in my mom's basement all hours of the day and night.

I had the same mindset and attitude towards work that many entry level workers have today. I wondered, "How can I get paid for doing as little as possible?"

My parents didn't make me get a job. I grew up working in the family business during the summers making $50 a week as a camp counselor. But that was cool because that's all the spending money I needed for the weekend. Heck, I would even have some left over. Do you see that? Can you see my lack of forethought about the future? $50 a week was all I needed for the coming weekend. That's as far as I looked ahead. My parents were paying for college; my car; my gas; my spending money... everything. It was great. Or so I thought at the time, but it wasn't preparing me for the train of reality. I didn't even see the train coming directly at me full steam... just around the bend in the tracks.

I'm telling you this because I want you to know that these immature and unrealistic mindsets about how the world works are not unique to "your generation". I think they are human! It's just that these current times have given rise to such a vast amount of information, resources and opportunity that things that the older generations would have loved, just weren't available so they had to get out there and figure it out. I don't think they were incredibly virtuous (as a whole), I just think they were limited with the resources and therefore had to figure it out quicker.

You are now confronted with having to get a job to make some money to begin to pay for more and more of your life. It's called growing up. It's a good thing. Many of you reading this book, may still have someone paying for most of your life. That's cool, but it may not be preparing you for the train of reality that's coming.

Soon you will be facing questions like what job should I get and how do I go about getting it? How do I compete for the job? How do I get promoted? How do I get a pay raise? How do I get ahead in life? How long will I have to wait until I can have what I want? Why can't I have it all now?

These are questions that I never spent much time thinking about. I just thought it would all work out. I just needed to find a "job" and the rest would naturally take care of itself. Well, I was wrong. The future won't "just take care of itself" if that means you actually achieve your goals. True; talent and skill will get you a job and a job will bring in money for you, but at some point, you're going to want more than your natural talent and skill can provide. To reach this "more" you're going to need a thoughtful strategy and diligent execution along with some patience, humility and some luck.

"I find that the harder I work, the more luck I
seem to have."

THOMAS JEFFERSON
*(America's 3rd President, statesman, diplomat, lawyer and Founding
Father of The United States of America)*

This book is my attempt to give you a handful of principles about how the world works and several practical tools so you can dominate the workplace quicker and have a huge head start on your competition. This book is meant to help you avoid the train of reality that is coming toward you. This is NOT a book about how you can change the world. It's NOT a book about finding your purpose in life and living in your passion every day. It's NOT a book telling you how awesome you are and how you can do anything you set your mind to. It's NOT a book about how to be happy. That's not helpful or practical for anyone at the beginning of a journey. There are books and speeches written about how your generation will change the future. This is not that book.

This book is more about how you can win in a marketplace that is rapidly changing around you. I can't save you from this life smackdown. I can't hold back the train of reality that is coming. The struggle is a necessary part of your preparation. Success in life requires thick skin and some life scars. However, this book can help you prepare for it. This book has given you exclusive insights into the minds of your bosses and the people that are out ahead of you on life's path and that are now making decisions for you and whether or not they should help you move forward in your life. This book has shown you how to stand out in the crowded competition of the workplace. This book has shown you how to get any job you're qualified for and how to dominate your competition and get promoted, and make more money. This book is your map to Just Don't Suck. If you follow the plan consistently and courageously, you can move quickly through this life process and avoid getting stuck in the valley of a life that is just "good enough".

Now, get out there and **JUST DON'T SUCK!**

If this book has been helpful for you,
please go to www.amazon.com and
give it a review.

If you have any questions, please shoot me an email and I'd be glad to answer them. My email address is clay@claystaires.com